CANOEING

by John Brailsford and
Stephen Baker

CANOEING

John Brailsford and Stephen Baker

Oxford Illustrated Press 1977

Acknowledgements

The authors wish to express their particular thanks and appreciation to Mike Clark for his excellent photography. Additional thanks go to Mr Gerald Perry for the line drawings and to Rev. Bob Shepton and the boys of St. Davids School, Llandudno for the interviews. Thanks also are expressed to the B.C.U. and club secretaries who kindly returned completed questionnaires.

Finally we would like to thank David Wain, Chairman of the Welsh Canoeing Association for his interest and encouragement in the final production of this book.

© Oxford Illustrated Press, John Brailsford, Stephen Baker and Mike Clark, 1977

Printed and Bound by Chapel River Press, Andover, Hampshire

ISBN 0 902280 41 4

The Oxford Illustrated Press Limited, Shelley Close, Headington, Oxford

Contents

Introduction

This book is the result of a discussion between the authors on the theme of what canoeing means to them. Each has a varied and contrasting canoeing experience but both currently enjoy an area of Wales rich in exciting and demanding canoeing water. Arising from these experiences we both feel that the element of the unknown potential hazard adds a dimension to canoeing without which the sport would not be quite the same.

We have deliberately limited the scope of the book to the areas which often form a spring-board for the novice to become initiated into the sport. Each area is illustrated with exciting action shots hopefully conveying some of the atmosphere which paddlers commonly experience. An attempt has been made to present a broad spectrum of canoeing water starting at the lower levels, on gentle rapids with small gradients, where the novices receive their first thrills, and then moving onto the larger rivers such as the Colorado which test even our most talented paddlers. Within each section we have also treated the non-competitive and competitive aspects separately in the belief that competition is not for all, but that for those who seek competition, canoeing offers it in a most spectacular way.

Although certain aspects tend to be seasonal, canoeing in one form or another, takes place all the year round. The summer tends to be down river expedition time when canoeing and camping become even more pleasurable as the cool of the water provides a welcome change from the rays of the sun. The bulk of Slalom competitions are held in the spring and autumn when hopefully, more water is flowing down the rivers. Winter tends to be devoted to down river trips utilising the spate conditions of our mountainous regions, and to white water races which provide competitive training for the summer slalomists. Surfing is truly an all-year-round activity; Surf conditions on our best beaches depend on the strength and direction of the wind. Our unpredictable weather, about which many non-canoeists complain bitterly, can produce good surfing conditions at any time.

Whichever aspect of the sport stimulates the novice to take up canoeing, we whole-heartedly recommend that when he has made his decision that he goes through one of the many excellent canoeing clubs listed in the Appendix. So strong is this feeling that a random selection of clubs was contacted in order to quantify the range of canoeing facilities they offered.

The majority of clubs occupied their own premises which often secured access to local water. A considerable number owned a pool of equipment for use by their newer members. In a few cases, canoe moulds were available and with the help of more experienced club members a newcomer is able to produce his own canoe or kayak at a fraction of the cost of one built professionally. Of course the club notice board is often a source of second-hand equipment but what is probably more important is the availability of advice on the choice, design and purchase of equipment which is invaluable to the novice and which is freely available at a club. Notwithstanding the advantages of equipment source, coaching and competitive organisation, most clubs serve their membership in other ways. Much work is done at club level on the ever-looming problem of water access; links with governing and other sporting bodies are formed and insurance is facilitated. By no means least the social life of a canoeing club, like any other type of club, is not only composed of active paddlers but also their friends and families, parents and former canoeists whose colourful and often somewhat exaggerated experiences make for humorous and invigorating club-house chat.

You learn by *doing* and a club encourages this approach.

Equipment

To start canoeing you need only three items of equipment: a canoe, a paddle and a life jacket. You then need an accessible stretch of water.

Simple as this statement may seem, the novice is faced with an immediate dilemma of choice. Canoeing has grown out of the original Eskimo kayak from Greenland and the open, Canadian canoe used by the North American Indian, to a sport with many aspects. These vary from touring in the broadest sense to competition, including slalom, white water racing, surfing and canoe sailing. For each activity, different specialist equipment is being developed and modified constantly to give improved performance. To follow the development of any aspect, it is necessary to understand the basic design principles of canoes and accessories.

It is hoped that the following factors concerning various types of equipment, design characteristics and principal uses, will lead to such understanding. We are also anxious that you make an economic purchase which suits your purpose.

Canoe or Kayak

Canoe, or 'C' boats, are propelled by kneeling occupants using single-bladed paddles. There are 'open' canoes which are still used extensively for carrying equipment for touring in Sweden and Canada. Open canoes are less suitable for use in rough water and for these conditions a 'deck' has been incorporated which makes the craft more water tight. Canadian canoes are still very popular, particularly in North America and with family groups. This is because of their carrying capacity when for example camping gear is to be carried without the support of a vehicle.

A slightly different type of Canadian canoe has evolved for competition and white water and these are discussed separately in their relevant sections.

Eskimo Kayak

As the name implies, this type of craft originated

A popular and enjoyable way of descending the Ardèche in Southern France is by open Canadian. The size of these C2s makes them very stable and difficult to capsize, which is why crash hats are not being worn. These canoes are still widely used on the lakes of Canada and Sweden and there is ample room for carrying camping equipment.

with the Eskimos and was introduced into Britain at the beginning of the nineteenth century. The kayak is propelled by a seated occupant using a double-bladed paddle. Kayaks, which are also referred to as 'K' boats, are sometimes known as 'doubles' (K2s), which means that they are paddled by two occupants. The single (K1) is the most common and most frequently used class of kayak, but in passing, it is interesting to know that there is a special class of racing kayak carrying four people, the 'K4'.

Boat Design

Whichever kind of craft you choose, there are some basic design characteristics which deter-

Left: *A white water racing C1: note the deep bow for cutting through waves. C1 paddlers tend to be more unstable in their boats than other paddlers because they are kneeling, and their centre of gravity is therefore higher.*

Below: *A paddler shooting the Bickleigh Mill Weir on the River Exe using a K1 with a rudder attachment and an asymmetric blade.*

This slalom kayak, showing its banana shaped hull, is highly manoeuvrable.

mine performance in terms of suitability for a particular class of the sport and its manoeuvrability or speed.

Rocker

This term describes the long profile of the boat hull from bow to stern. In other words, how flat or curved the keel is. The shape of the keel will determine how straight a course the boat will maintain. A craft with no rocker, i.e. a flat keel, is paddled in a straight line more easily. By contrast, a boat with a lot of rocker, banana shaped, is difficult to paddle on a straight course but it is highly manoeuvrable.

Length

The length of a boat is closely related to the amount of rocker it is given. A craft designed for speed will be a lot longer than one designed for manoeuvrability and it will have little or no rocker. Obviously, length is influenced by the number of paddles it is to carry and the nature of water over which it will be paddled, K4s, for example, do not become involved with rocky, white water rivers but are used on still water.

Cross Section

The cross section of a hull profile of canoe or kayak also determines its performance. A 'V' section produces speed and is commonly seen in long boats with no rocker.

A 'U' section produces the facility to move sideways and it is associated with the shorter craft used for slalom and general white water paddling.

Experimentation is also taking place in the sphere of surf kayak design where a flat hull form enables the paddler to slide and rotate on the face of a wave.

Buoyancy

To avoid confusion, we use the term here as being the volume of a craft when sealed with a spray deck cover fitted to the cockpit. When choosing a kayak it is particularly important that you choose one suitable for your body weight. A buoyant boat is one which rides high on the water with the occupant in position and this makes it more comfortable to handle. A boat which has its gunwhales awash is most difficult to handle and implies that the paddler has outgrown his boat.

Fixed Buoyancy

This refers to the means by which air is trapped in the craft so that, in the event of a capsize, the boat still floats. Air can be trapped in containers such as car inner tubes, plastic balls, empty sherry or squash containers or similar discarded but intact vessels. Most common fixed buoyancy is provided by blocks of polystyrene which also give support to the deck, and are lined vertically from the foot rest to bow and from behind the cockpit to stern. Whichever means you use it is most important that the method of securing it within the boat is both sound and fool proof. Buoyancy which merely floats out of a capsized kayak is of no use to anyone. The more space the buoyancy occupies, the less water can enter. This ensures an easy swim ashore and emptying process.

Deck Fittings

Many canoeists have developed their own ideas and devices for deck fittings. Some are more relevant to sea canoeing whilst others aid rescue or a teaching situation. Of all the fittings to be seen, the means by which one hangs on to the capsized craft is the most important.

A new G.R.P. kayak, delivered from the manufacturer, will be fitted with a loop of synthetic cord attached to the bow and stern. This fulfils the need one has of being able to hang on to the boat but it is most uncomfortable if one is in the unfortunate position of having to swim far with the kayak, as at sea. The loop can be made more effective by threading a wooden toggle or plastic ball on to the line.

Some canoeists fit lines from bow or stern loops to the cockpit and this certainly eases the handling problem. Unless these lines are securely anchored and checked for tension then a slack or loose line may ensnare the canoeist in the water, or create problems for the occupant acting as a rescuer.

Spray Decks

Canoes and kayaks designed for rough water generally have a small cockpit area into which the paddler fits. Water is prevented from entering the cockpit by an elasticated cover which fits both the rim edge of the cockpit and the waist of the canoeist.

Spray decks are made from two basic types of material. It is relatively easy and cheap to make your own spray cover from waterproofed bri-nylon. A more durable and effective cover may be made from nylon-backed neoprene which is, with care, within the skill of the home craftsman.

Whichever type is used, a loop must be fixed firmly to the front of the cover to enable the canoeist to pull it from the cockpit.

Canoe Construction

There are three major methods of canoe construction normally used in Britain. There are other industrial methods in the course of development, but these are of little direct interest to the potential home or club based builder.

The first mode of construction is the 'lath and canvas' form. As the terms imply, a frame is made from timber and marine ply sheet, over which is stretched either canvas or PVC material. It is a fairly straight forward process requiring few tools, given a concern for good finishing and careful marking out techniques. A lath and canvas boat is well suited to estuary, still water and rivers without undue hazard in the shape of complicated boulder fields or falls. They were used in slalom competition up to the advent of the G.R.P. development which really came in the early 1960s.

The Littledyke, or 'Kayel' approach was devised by a craft teacher, Ken Littledyke. He joined strips of marine ply wood, which were cut to precise patterned form. The join is made by 'stitching' the strips with copper wire loops, which are twisted, using pliers, to close the gap, and sealed with fibreglass tape wet out with polyester resin. This is a simple technique requiring thought and care and a minimum of equipment. This same method is applied to the manufacture of sailing dinghies as well as canoes.

Glass-Reinforced-Plastic or, commonly, fibreglass construction now accounts for the majority of modern canoes and kayaks. Ocean going craft are also made from the materials as are some cars like the Reliant Scimitar. This supports the value of glassfibre construction as being strong, light and very resiliant or resistant to impact. This robust material can be handled at home and to begin, you need to hire a mould from either a club or school source, or you may hire one from a commercial firm. Many of these concerns advertise in canoe publications and will be known to experienced builders or club paddlers.

Labour is the next problem. Two people can and have built boats, but it is true to say that within limits, a group of up to eight workers is more efficient.

Particular care is needed to see that the chemical components are handled properly and that the working area is well ventilated. Adhere strictly to the recommended mixing details and other safety factors concerning the components, the reactant or catalyst being the most damaging to skin. In all events, do take advice before

4

embarking on glassfibre construction. The cost of a self-built boat is currently about one third to one quarter the cost of a manufactured one. However, it is only fair to say that unless you have an expert involved during your construction, you will not achieve that quality of finish associated with a professional product.

Paddles

Paddles vary in design and materials, which in turn influence cost. To the competitor, the cost of a good set of blades can amount to a quarter of the cost of his craft. To the novice and modest performer, this level of expenditure is not necessary. Quality apart, the following features should be considered.

Length

A paddle designed to facilitate handling skills will be shorter than one designed for speed of forward propulsion. Hence one may hear reference to a 'slalom' paddle or a 'racing' blade.

If you extend your arm vertically and you can curl the first joint around the tip of the upper blade then that double paddle is suitable for you in slalom. For other paddling, a set of blades a few inches longer is more suitable.

A Canadian paddle with only one blade and fixed with a 'T' handle should be approximately two thirds the height of the intended user. Canadian paddles are normally supplied with the 'T' piece handle separate for you to measure and fix.

Shape

Again, the shape of blade varies according to the intended usage. Flat blades are generally used by novices and there are several advantages for such a choice. First and foremost, a flat blade mounted in a plastic covered shaft or 'loom' is the least expensive buy. They are quite strong and easy to drill out and replace if broken. The main disadvantage of the flat blade is its 'slippage' during a stroke in the water. This means that as the paddle is pulled through the water, a considerable amount of water slips off the blade and power is lost.

To counteract this slippage, the curved blade has been developed, but this increases the cost. Even with a curved blade there is still some slippage occurring over the edges of the blade. Spoon shapes were then introduced with a curve in two planes and are even more expensive. These are largely confined to racing paddles. Fibreglass blades of the spoon type also tend to 'flutter' in white water technique strokes which leaves the curved, wood paddle as the most popular choice for general and slalom work.

The loom of the paddle is also important since

This shot of a C1 competitor clearly shows the Canadian paddle. Note the 'T'-shaped handle.

the user must grip this firmly enough to counteract rotation, yet with comfort. Looms are either round or oval. The round loom is found on the metal product and the oval on wood construction. The ovalness gives the user a feel of the shaft related to the angle of the blade without having to look for this. You can create an oval form on a metal loom by marking the handling area and carefully pressing it in a good wood workers vice, making sure that the squeezing is done to match the face of the blades which are set at right angles to each other. Once you have acquired basic paddling skill you will soon wish to buy and use an oval-shafted paddle.

This problem does not arise with the Canadian paddle to the same extent. It is the shape and comfort of the 'T' handle which must be achieved.

The white water provides little support for this kayak which sinks below to the firm tongue of dark green water seen above the gate. This paddler is seen wearing a lifejacket which is partially inflated. It is obvious from the tee shirt that the weather is pleasant.

Life Jacket or Buoyancy Aid

A life jacket is a buoyant safety device which, only when inflated, automatically turns an unconscious victim face uppermost and supports him in that position. This is a subject which is widely discussed but the point made here about inflated performance is often overlooked. Most canoeists agree that to paddle with a life jacket inflated is most awkward and because of this it is used in the flat, deflated form. As such it becomes an *AID*, not a life jacket. However, if one is at sea or expecting a long spell in the water, then the life jacket can be inflated. It automatically becomes invalid if the victim is not conscious, in which case a rescuer should inflate the life jacket.

A single purpose buoyancy aid merely assists in floatation. These garments are sold in 'slip over' or 'zip-front opening' forms. They are made from nylon-based material and carry vertically supported columns of solid foam, buoyant and relatively indestructible, to give a minimum of six kilogrammes aid. These aids are favoured by most of today's competitors, in all branches of white water sport. They allow freedom of movement and are compact. They are also quite warm, acting as an armless anorak and they will protect the upper body against knocks from other boats or natural obstacles. Being completely free from the problem of puncturing we recommend this type of buoyancy aid for the proficient paddler.

Body Protection

We will describe some of the popular types of clothing used to protect the canoeist from either cold or physical contact, and work from head to feet.

The rules of slalom competition and white water racing dictate that a crash hat must be worn during events. It is prudent to continue this habit in any activity involving agitated water, river or sea, since the roughness stems from underlying physical features such as rocks or shelving beach. All these, together with overhanging trees, make for painful contact. On still water and less serious situations the dangers are reduced and therefore the decision may be reversed.

During cold weather, some additional form of insulation for the head is most effective and comfortable. The head is an area where there is no vaso constriction of the blood vessels in the cold, which exists in the rest of the body. Therefore, to minimise the heat loss, a woollen hat worn under the crash hat is of great benefit. If it covers the ears, so much the better; but do remove the bobbles from the top!

In warm conditions many canoeists prefer to wear only a tee shirt under the buoyancy aid. This

Team work is nowhere more important than in a C2. This pair, competing in a down river event at Monschau in West Germany, demonstrate the effectiveness of co-ordinate balance when negotiating a grade 3 rapid. Both paddlers are wearing a well-insulated yet flexible nylon overjacket.

is mainly to counteract the high level of ultra violet rays reflected from the surface of the water, which is similar to snow in this effect.

In the cold, the problem of body insulation assumes greater importance. Some wear the neoprene 'wet suit', which although warm when wet, offers some resistance to upper body movement because of its cut. This becomes particularly noticeable around the arms and pectoral area of the upper chest. Others prefer a 'dry suit', which is also known as a 'seal suit', made from thin latex rubber and worn over clothing of wool which retains warmth even when wet, and it stays soft. The dry suit seals at cuffs, neck and waist to prevent water entering. A dry suit can be made at home from a kit and is quite economic and efficient but demands careful treatment. With such care a suit should last from three to four seasons.

Nylon anoraks, worn over wool, are reasonably effective. There are now specially cut 'cagjaks' for canoeing, which have close fitting wrist and neck seals. This type of garment has one major advantage over the rubber dry suit in that it is more durable and less prone to tearing.

Although theoretically the lower half of the body should remain dry, this is theory only. Particularly in surf, one always ends up with some water in the boat, either via the spray deck or via seams in the craft itself. Water is not the only problem. Prolonged activity in white water involves considerable chaffing of the legs against the hull surfaces. Neoprene trousers or a 'Long John' offer the best, but most expensive solution. Old jeans are acceptable in summer, but old, wool cloth 'bags' are warmer in winter. In the event of a swim the wet suit garments score both for warmth and the buoyancy they afford. We favour a combination of a wet-suit type garment for the lower body and either the cagjak or 'seal suit', with wool underwear for the upper body. Some fibre-pile garments are also useful.

Finally we come to the feet. Cold apart, the feet need protection from sharp objects outside the kayak and the needle splinter forms from the fibreglass itself. 'Wet' boots, with or without an integral sole are a luxury. They can be made at home, using a sock as a pattern and joining two halves to make each bootee, and they are not expensive. However, almost as effective are gym shoes, but they must be tied on with extra security around the ankles, as the water tries very hard to suck them off. In winter, a pair of wool socks will make life a little more comfortable and ski socks are very cosy.

This group of paddlers, seen inspecting a rapid on the Colorado, shows a variety of summer dress. Note the footwear, spray covers, buoyancy aids and crash helmet.

Repairs

Little will be said at this stage about the major repair or re-building problem since familiarity with construction in the fullest sense will be needed. Suffice to say that several canoeists have succeeded in joining two separated halves of kayak successfully, if only to be used on surf and 'bump and scrape' river trips.

Temporary repair during a trip is another matter since urgent and effective waterproofing is needed to complete the trip. A fibreglass boat can be repaired using wide, ultra-violet sensitive tape, but this is expensive. We have found that household plumbing and glazing tape of the 'Sylglass' type works well. Both these products stick to wet surfaces.

If the surface can be dried, waterproof plastic insulating tape often holds. If a patch can be placed both inside and outside the damage, the effect of the 'sandwich' is good.

Repair to canvas is reasonably straight forward in that one can switch the rent and cover it with a suitable patch of canvas or even a simple carpet tape or 'elastoplast' strapping. The canvas should be as dry as possible.

Above: *By the number of repairs visible on the deck of this boat, perhaps it was time to retire. However, the wonders of fibreglass render this repair a real possibility.*

Transport

Group equipment is often carried on a canoe trailer. There are many types available and one matches design to precise purpose. It is often useful to incorporate some sort of box for stowing paddles and wet gear.

Individuals carry one, two and often three boats on a roof rack. There are certain features of the design of roof racks that should be considered seriously. There is tremendous air pressure upon the boats whilst in transit, and it is therefore wise to choose a rack with as many points of contact and support as possible. A ladder rack, with eight separate supports and clamps fitting the gutter of the car is good. To this basic fitting, one may fix additional framework to support the type and number of boats normally carried. Canoes should fit snugly and not move about.

Equally important to the fixing of the roof rack is the securing of the boats to *both* car and rack. The law is not on your side if you fail to fix your load securely, to say nothing of the personal expense involved. Use strong nylon cord, say five millimetre diameter, and tie the knots correctly. Clove hitches, or round turn with half hitches, rather than the famous, self-untying 'Granny

Below: *A major down river expedition is often only as successful as the planning and organisation that precedes it. Here is a typical behind-the-scenes shot of 'Colorado' preparation.*

9

A female slalomist clearly enjoying Olympic competition at Augsburg (1972). Note the excellence of her personal dress.

knot', should be used. Tie separate lines from bow and stern to the bumpers of the car from each boat on the rack; you will then arrive intact.

What to Buy

We hope that the material in this chapter has given you the important factors to consider concerning equipment. However, please bear in mind the advice we gave at the outset, that you need only three pieces of equipment to start.

We recommend that you select a general purpose, fibreglass constructed, slalom-type kayak which can be used for all the types of canoe sport covered in this book.

Buy a flat-bladed paddle with a metal loom which will suffice your needs for at least one season. Paddles tend to be replaced regularly in any case.

The advantages of a buoyancy aid, in our opinion and experience slightly outweigh those of the life jacket.

Do take advice before you rush out to buy. If at all possible, join a club and there you will receive all the expert guidance and advice you require. If a club is not accessible, then seek advice from other canoeists who have wide experience. It is all too easy to be persuaded that the latest design of slalom kayak for top class competition is for you, when what you really need is a more substantial, maybe even second-hand boat. All canoe sportsmen will be willing to offer advice or at least direct you towards someone who is better experienced who can be of real value to you. Spend in haste; regret at leisure.

Finally, mark all your property clearly and consider taking out either the B.C.U. insurance cover or ask your parents if they have the sort of policy to which your canoe gear may be added.

Wild Water Canoeing

Wild water canoeing is an exciting and vital heading which conjures up for some a descent of the mighty Colorado, while for others a memorable and enjoyable expedition down the Wye or Severn. Whatever your age, sex, or physical ability, there is a wild water river somewhere which will be a match for you. Of course, not all rivers are suitable or available for canoeists to use.

Some are not deep enough and only in times of heavy rainfall is there enough volume of water available. It is only our larger rivers, which the geographer might classify as 'old aged', with gentle gradients and whose volume is maintained by their many tributaries that are suitable for canoeing at any time. Unfortunately these rivers are often popular and expensive fishing haunts,

This shot of a down river race through the Serpents Tail on the River Dee shows the unmistakable love-hate relationship between canoeist and water. The paddler is using a glassfibre blade fitted to a wooden loom.

and access to them is by no means automatic or legal. The time is rapidly approaching where canoeists, like fishermen, must be prepared to pay for the use of rivers in order that both sportsmen might co-exist harmoniously.

How then can rivers best be described so that an interpretation of the 'details' is straightforward, accurate and universally meaningful? Initially canoeists are interested in the overall standard of the river, including the technical difficulty of rapids and their frequency. In this context it is useful to categorise rivers into one of two kinds. The first we shall call 'novice' rivers which have gentle gradients and relatively slow rates of current. In these rivers, rapids, which may occur frequently, are technically easy to descend and are followed by extensive stretches of flat water. The second type of river falls into the advanced category and includes all those rivers beyond the

Left: Many novices spend their first canoeing hours on flat water where basic boat handling skills are learned and consolidated. Below: Although ferocious there are no objective hazards such as boulders in this rapid. The best way of handling this kind of water (grade 4-5) is to paddle as hard as possible. Two rescuers are seen in the background ready to give assistance if required.

capabilities of novice canoeists. Within this group fit the worlds largest rivers suitable for descent by kayak, and two characteristic features of this type are a steep gradient and a large volume of water.

Within each river group, individual rapids can be described by an existing river grading system. Since there are no hard and fast rules for grading a rapid, this system has in the past been much abused, and therefore it has not been uncommon for two canoeists to grade a rapid differently. This discrepancy of grading does seem to be less pronounced between very experienced canoeists, however. The system employs a numerical scale from 1 to 6, where the latter implies water conditions which are a distinct risk to life.

Grade 1
Water moving at a rate of 2-3 mph over an undulating river bed where any descent route is acceptable.

Grade 2
A rapid with a steepening gradient which levels out almost immediately where the water flows into a V shaped or series of V shaped channels which define a descent route.

Grade 3
A longer rapid with a marked fall in the level of the river bed and with obvious channels of descent. There may be interspersed or submerged rocks which provide objective dangers. During a descent a kayak may become fully submerged with water splashing occasionally in the face of the canoeist. In this grade there will be a noteable increase in the volume of water compared with grade 2.

Grade 4
Wild and turbulent water produces complicated features such as stopper waves, stack waves interspersed with boulders which force a canoeist to manoeuvre his craft through the rapid. The volume and speed of water is greater than a grade 3. Possible resting places below the rapid are scarce. A canoeist may become fully submerged with waves passing over his head on occasions.

Grade 5
Heavy torrents of water rushing down steep gradients where the overall appearance is white.

Pauline Goodwin in a down river race on the Tryweryn in North Wales. Since the water authority has kindly released large quantities of water from an upstream dam this has made the Tryweryn one of the best competitive rivers in Britain. Pauline is descending a grade 4 rapid where there is a notable drop in the river levels, and where considerable manoeuvrability is required.

13

Two shots of the river Tryweryn. Rivers such as this are particularly dangerous in high spate when the water level interferes with the branches of trees. Partly submerged trees are one of the canoeist's most serious hazards.

Above: *Some more adventurous paddlers brave the consequences of obstacles such as this fall. Often the depth of water below a drop of this height is adequate for a plunging descent but it would only be a foolish paddler who would make the attempt without first inspecting the rapid from the bank. The higher the inspection point above a rapid the better. Gorge surroundings lend themselves to this aerial observation.* Below: *A female competitor on the Llangollen Town rapid is about to emerge from the turbulence. Darker areas of water support a buoyant boat whereas the white agitated water, containing a great deal of air, encircles a boat as we see here.*

The importance of rescue facilities present at particularly bad trouble spots is apparent here: canoeists are in trouble at Cowley Bridge Steps on the River Exe. Notorious rapids such as this are always manned by one or more rescuers. These men have either lost their crash hats during this incident or foolishly did not wear them.

A canoeist will frequently become screened from the view of onlookers by large waves and spray. There is no easing of the gradient for a considerable distance which renders the consequences of a capsize most unpleasant and not without some danger.

Grade 6

This has been occasionally termed the 'lucky grade', which means that you are lucky if you survive a descent intact. Not many of the British rivers exhibit this kind of ferocious water and those which do are confined to the mountainous regions. This kind of water, found in Britain only during periods of heavy and prolonged rainfall, is more commonly observed on the larger rivers of the world which depend on many tributaries for their water volume.

A grade for a rapid tells us something about a particular and often short stretch of water. However, there are other factors such as overhanging trees, low bridges, narrow and winding gorges and other objective hazards which although not included in the grading system are of immense importance to the canoeist. Therefore in the overall grading of a river, consider initially the gradient, which, with experience provides a fairly accurate prediction of the types of rapids to be encountered, and then the geography. Is it in a gorge where the escape might prove difficult? Are overhanging trees a prominent feature, or is it over open farm land where barbed wire might have been erected across the river to fence in cows and farm animals?

Skills

A novice river with an abundance of grade 2 rapids is an ideal place to put into practice those boat handling strokes which you have been shown on flat water. Ideally you will be able to roll (learnt in the club sessions at the swimming pool) in which case a mistake, manifested as a capsize, will be corrected quickly by a roll instead of a cold swim ashore.

One of the first skills to acquire is an understanding of when and how to present the hull of your boat to current. In order to have control over your kayak you must be moving at a different speed from the water beneath you. This means

Above: *The warm and clean water of a swimming pool provides ideal conditions for introducing basic skills. Here we see a beginner attempting an Eskimo roll. The resistance of the paddle blade on the water enables the canoeist to rotate at the other end of the loom. A most important prerequisite to acquiring this skill quickly, is a snugly fitting boat.*
Below: *A C1 paddler mid-way through a roll in a down river event at Llangollen. Note the shape of the canoe with a wide section located behind the cockpit which makes this a rather unstable craft.*

Jim Sibley of Britain, competing in a C1 at the World Championship down river at Bourg St. Maurice in France, is seen breaking through a standing wave in his white water racing canoe.

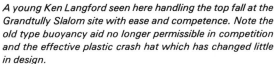

A young Ken Langford seen here handling the top fall at the Grandtully Slalom site with ease and competence. Note the old type buoyancy aid no longer permissible in competition and the effective plastic crash hat which has changed little in design.

that you may have to move faster or, equally effective, more slowly than the water. Turning your kayak on water involves the same principle of balance to that used on a bicycle, where a left-hand turn is achieved by leaning left and a right-hand turn by leaning right. In producing such a body lean in a kayak, implying that the lean must also incorporate the boat, then the aspect of the hull presented to the moving water will facilitate a turn and prevent a capsize.

Ferry Glides

This skill must be acquired early in your training session. It involves moving your kayak across a current without losing or gaining ground up or downstream. It is best learnt facing the current but must be quickly transferred to face downstream. In context, the skill is useful on a down river trip when you suddenly notice a danger area ahead of you, in which case you stop, by paddling backwards and then move your kayak across the current to align it with a safe passage.

Break Out

On the downstream side of every rock in a river is an area of slack water. In such places you can rest, or wait for your friends, while the current continues at great speed on either side of you. In order to enjoy the calm of an eddy, you must paddle your craft hard into it. Anticipate the current turning you round as the eddy, in effect, holds your bow, and lean accordingly into the turn.

Break outs are great fun and they add an extra dimension of enjoyment to a down river trip. The more proficient canoeist will still attempt break

Warm water, sun and canoes. An exciting adventure holiday for these teenage canoeists, mostly beginners, who come together for two weeks of fun in the gorges of Southern France. This makes a great introduction to canoe sport.

A portrait of tremendous enjoyment and excitement taken in the impressive gorge surroundings on the Ardèche in Southern France. A memorable holiday for anyone, why not try it?

outs in the higher grades of water and once these have been mastered forwards, then they will try them backwards.

Eddy Hopping

With the exception of the white water racing canoeist, few others will simply paddle on down a river without exhausting the possibilities of each rapid. Having just passed down the section, the more adventurous will try to paddle back up a rapid. This is not always easy to do and the best way is to paddle from an eddy behind one rock upstream, to another area of slack water. In many cases you will be able to continue in this fashion back to the top of the rapid for your second descent. Alternatively, if a rapid proves too powerful to paddle against, why not carry round and have another go?

Party Management

A natural progression from a practice session on a limited area of white water is a down river trip. Although for the novice these should be light hearted and enjoyable events (inspite of the possibility of a few spills), there are certain rules which must be obeyed.

The leader of the expedition should be familiar with the river and its potential hazards. Most coaches would agree that it would be a very unwise group leader who decided to take his party of novices on a river completely new to him. If there are potential danger areas then an inspection of these by the whole party is desirable.

20

The party may then observe how an experienced canoeist negotiates the difficulty before attempting it in their turn.

The party leader must convey to his group prior to the trip his signal system. Bear in mind that there is a great deal of noise in a rapid and it is often impossible to shout instructions above it. A widely used signal system is as follows. One arm or paddle raised means next man proceed. Arm out to right (observed by pupil in descent) means move to right; similarly, an arm out to left means move to left. Two arms raised means wait or stop. You may decide to modify or add to this system, which is fine; but keep all signals simple and meaningful to be effective.

It has been implied already that there should be single descents of rapids while the rest of the party wait upstream for their turn, then collect downstream following their descent. Collecting in this way is a convenient check on group numbers and also an accumulation of potential help for an individual who in some way requires assistance.

White water training inevitably produces an acquisition of skill and an enormous amount of thrill and enjoyment, but over and above that it slowly develops, for want of a better term, the 'solo concept'. Although an individual rarely canoes alone, essentially he is alone, in that his comrades can do little to help him if he gets into difficulties, particularly on rapids of Grade 3 and above. He must rely on his skill, judgement, his interpretation of the currents and his boat handling ability to solve the problems which the rivers pose for him.

A Challenge

Having served his apprenticeship on novice rivers, the proficient canoeist looks further afield in

The Grand Canyon support party ferries equipment from these large rafts to a rocky campsite. Not only do these rafts serve that purpose but these also act as a taxi service to those unfortunate canoeists who have lost their boats or irreparably damaged them.

This paddler is paddling in a white water racing Kayak. The high vertical bow designed for cutting through waves can be seen clearly. In this design, a V cross section hull makes it difficult to balance upright.

search of larger rivers and more technical rapids on which to test his ability. At this stage, many seek their thrills abroad on the larger rivers of Europe such as the Inn or Isere, or in America and Canada where rivers like the Colorado are in abundance.

These larger down river expeditions are of course not to be undertaken lightly; they need to be planned carefully with contingencies for each eventuality. The choice of equipment becomes a major factor; transportation and support parties must be given equal consideration and, in many cases, the actual river descent becomes the most 'relaxing' part of the expedition.

White Water Racing

Other paddlers seek their challenge in competition against the clock over a stretch of white water. White water racing is a demanding event both physically and perceptually. It is held over stretches of water ranging from three to eight miles where strength and stamina are obviously important. However, brawn without brain does not constitute a successful white water racing competitor. He must be alert and vigilant, constantly searching out the fastest and most direct line through hazardous boulder fields in heavy rapids, and avoiding the slowing effects of large eddies.

White water racing, principally a winter event, is in contrast to the slalom season and is used by many slalomists as part of their fitness training programme for the following season.

Seasonal Variations

It has already been mentioned that canoeing in some form is practised throughout the year. The canoeist therefore is faced with the environmental stresses of either cold ambient air, near freezing water or both. It is possible, of course, to canoe on the freezing Alpine rivers in France in blazing sunshine. To minimize the unpleasant and potentially dangerous effects of cold immersion, the canoeist must pay particular attention to the insulative value of his clothing. Unfortunately many neglect the potential dangers of this problem and consequently narrow their safety margin.

The ears, and in particular the ear canal (external auditory meatus) is an area of the head which is most sensitive to the effects of cold irrigation. Cold water entering the ear can cause a nystagmus which is an involuntary movement in the eye, and it is thought that this effect could interfere with performance to detrimental effect. An obvious precaution to take when canoeing on cold water therefore is to insulate the head.

Canoeists know only too well the unpleasant sensation of cold hands, indeed some suffer more than others, but few suffer no discomfort. Many have tried to reduce these effects by wearing gloves of various designs, but this idea has not been adopted universally because gloves lack the firmness of a direct hand-paddle contact. It is fortunate for the canoeist that man is adaptable

Peter and Ria Van Stipdonk of Holland competing in the down river event at Monschau. The vertical bow, raised fore deck and position of both paddlers amidships is clearly shown in this shot of a racing C2. Note the handle on the end of the paddle.

and if exposed frequently to extreme conditions of cold, becomes acclimatised. Therefore, to combat cold on your hands, expose them regularly in cold water and icy winds and although this is often painful and unpleasant, eventually there will be a noticeable reduction in the level of discomfort.

Equipment

Although equipment has been discussed generally in a preceding chapter, there are some items of special equipment which have been designed specifically for use in white water.

First and foremost is the white water racing kayak. This is longer than the slalom kayak, with practically no rocker and a V-shaped cross section to promote directional speed. There are also white water racing Canadian canoes which have similar design characteristics to racing kayaks. A racing C2 is seen in the photograph above.

For non competitive down river trips, a slalom-type boat with its pronounced rocker and smooth

U-shaped hull for manoeuvrability is a good choice. A buoyant boat with a reasonably high deck will ride high in heavier turbulent water.

Generally speaking the rest of the equipment used in white water canoeing is the same as that previously described.

Access

In the past, access has been a topic dreaded by most canoeists. Rivers, unlike the public highways, are private property and according to law and social rules, one must ask for permission to pass over private property.

A great deal of progress has been made in the past and many landowners are quite willing for canoeists, providing they are responsible and tidy individuals, to use their river. However, some stretches of river are owned by fishing clubs and

Canoeists frequently are able to observe wild life at very close quarters. It may be mallard, oystercatchers or heron feeding or, as we see in this shot, the wild Burro which abounds in North America.

permission to use these stretches is often difficult to secure. The most difficult time of all is of course in the fishing season. Many fishing clubs have realised that their past policy of no canoeing at any time is selfish and unreasonable, and have agreed to closed-season canoeing.

The root of the problem is the price you pay for your sport. It is well known that certain stretches of some good salmon rivers are available to each fisherman paying a sum which occasionally runs into four figures. The canoeist at present pays very little and often nothing for using a river. Of course the fishermen are taking something from the river, and some of their costs go towards restocking. The canoeist on the other hand takes nothing. Often restrictions are imposed on the number of fishermen that may use a stretch of water. This can be done by limiting the number of permits or by raising 'rod' fees to a level which reduces numbers and stratifies fishermen by wealth.

From the point of view of the fisherman, who has paid an extortionate amount of money to fish a particular stretch of water, the sight of a canoeist or, worse, a party of canoeists approaching his pool is often unacceptable. This problem still exists and it will not be solved immediately. However, a polite and friendly approach, a willingness to wait, to pass on the other side or even portage round quietly, will help indirectly to solve the access problem. If canoeists are generally regarded as considerate and co-operative sportsmen by fishermen, half the battle is won.

However, access will only come universally either by an Act of Parliament or by payment of fees. After all, one has to pay the landowner for using his field as a campsite, so why not pay him for being allowed to use his river? At the present time a system of payment or licences is not readily available but thoughts on these lines are being widely expressed.

In the meantime enjoy your canoeing but at the same time, please strictly adhere to the country code, and, what is more important, preach it to others. It takes a long time and a tremendous amount of goodwill to create a favourable reputation, but this is quickly eroded by careless and thoughtless behaviour.

Slalom Canoeing

What is Slalom?

Slalom, a term borrowed from skiing, is one competitive aspect of canoeing that can be considered as a sport in its own right. Its aim is to test and rank an individual's canoeing skills, at speed, in agitated water. To do this a competitor is timed over a short stretch of white water as he passes through 'gates' en route to the finish. A gate, consisting of two poles of different colours suspended from cord, spans the course and is positioned over particularly tricky parts of the current. There may be up to thirty gates on a slalom course, each numbered, which must be attempted in numerical order.

A canoeist must paddle his boat through the gate forwards or in reverse and the direction might be downstream or upstream. Above each gate on a square board is the number, and if a gate is to be taken in reverse (that is the stern of the boat entering the gate first), a letter 'R' is displayed on a separate square board adjacent to the gate number. A diagonal line through the gate number (and through the letter R if it is a reverse gate), indicates to the competitor that he is approaching the gate from the wrong direction. In addition to this system the colour of the poles also indicates correct presentation to the competitor. Red and white poles are always left of the cockpit and green and white poles always to the right.

If a paddler touches part of a gate as he passes through it he collects penalty seconds which are added to the time it takes him to reach the finish. The competitor with the fastest total time is declared the winner.

There are two main types of slalom. The first is a natural slalom which is held on a rapid section of a river. In Britain there are many sections of our

This competitor is carefully aligning his kayak for a clear passage through this reverse gate. Note the clear numbering system employed at all slaloms.

larger rivers on which slaloms are held at different times of the year. There are many sections of some smaller rivers that also serve as attractive venues. However, our erratic weather variations render these smaller rivers unreliable and unpredictable.

The second slalom category, termed artificial, is divided into three types: a weir slalom, a 'controlled flow' slalom and a purpose-built slalom. A weir slalom, as the name suggests, is held below an artificial weir where gates are suspended over the turbulent water. Most of our weir slaloms are held on the River Thames at places such as Shepperton or Marsh Lock. The advantage of a weir competition from the slalomist's point of view is that his embarkation and disembarkation point are at the same spot. That is to say he can launch his kayak, paddle to the start, compete and paddle back to the same spot without having to carry his boat. There are some rivers, on the other hand, where, having finished, canoeists have to carry their boats over a quarter of a mile back to the start.

A controlled flow slalom may be held at a weir or on a river but the **common** characteristic is that the volume of water **is controlled** higher upstream

Both these competitors will collect a ten second penalty: the Belgian girl in the left-hand photo for hitting the green pole (always on her right), the C1 paddler in the right-hand photo for hitting the red pole (always on the left). Further contact with the same pole while in the gate imposes no further penalty.

by sluice gates. One of Britain's best slalom sites of this type is on the River Tryweryn in Wales. A consistent flow of water throughout the duration of a two-day event is most important for valid competition. One of the advantages of this type of artificial slalom over the others is that the turbulent water produces relatively constant and predictable patterns of movement. The turbulence produced at a weir site on the other hand is random in the form of 'boils' and whirlpools which are not predictable. The controlled flow situation would seem to be the most desirable and economical type of slalom, particularly when compared with the last artificial type, the purpose-built slalom course. As you can imagine, it is very expensive to build an artificial river for the sole

An early shot of David Mitchell competing in a slalom at Builth Wells in a K.W. Kayak. Although obeying the rules by wearing a crash hat, the type he is using does not offer the same degree of protection as the plastic type.

purpose of producing turbulent conditions suitable for a slalom. It cost the Germans over one million pounds to construct such a course for the slalom canoeing event at the 1972 Olympic Games at Augsburg.

From the types of slalom, we next consider the variety of events. Events are categorised into boat types, and within each of these there is a further sub-division into men's and women's events in all but Canadian singles.

The most popular type of slalom boat is the K1: the K stands for Kayak and the figure indicates the number of people in it. A Kayak is propelled by a seated canoeist using a double-bladed paddle.

The alternative class of boat is the Canadian canoe, of which there are two types: the C1 and C2. In the C1 a single canoeist kneeling in a cockpit amidships propells the canoe with a single-bladed paddle 'Indian style'. The C2 is a larger craft with a canoeist kneeling at either end, also paddling with single-bladed paddles.

Finally there is the team event, which many hold to be the most exciting and skillful of all, in which three competitors race over the course working closely together whilst simultaneously avoiding each other.

Slalom development

Slalom canoeing is one of Britain's most rapidly developing sports, with the introduction of the fibreglass Kayak in the early Sixties marking the

An early shot of Raymond Calverley (1968) later to become British Champion (1975) competing on a weir slalom at Shepperton on the River Thames. Note the large number of gates in a relatively short area. Sluice gates have been opened on the far side while those to the left of the picture remained closed.

Speed linked with a well-chosen line often avoids the difficulties which others experienced at slower speeds. Here a paddler skillfully negotiates a gate on the notorious Bala Mill fall on the Tryweryn River.

The C1 paddlers have to wrestle and handle the same current and course as the K1 paddlers but with only a single-blade paddle.

An early shot of Dave Mitchell competing at Builth Wells on a typical grade 3 rapid.

birth of modern slalom competition. Although World Championship slaloms date back into the 1950s the sport was not included in the Olympic programme until 1972. As with most sports, individuals have dominated pole positions for many years, and the competitor which many will remember with admiration on the slalom scene from the mid-1960s to the mid-1970s is David Mitchell. Not only was he a skillful, strong and aggressive competitor, but his improvement over ten years matched the rapid development in slalom skills occurring in Europe. The supreme moment in his career in retrospect must have been a silver medal at the World Championships in 1970, but unfortunately he was not able to match the skill of the East Europeans at Munich.

The Mitchell era, now over, has been replaced by younger blood in better canoes who, having been taught and bred on 'big rivers', accept our best slalom rivers as the norm.

Although never lacking in the spirit, determination and dedication for competition, the British slalomist is at one major disadvantage over his European counterpart, and that is the availability of white water. The glacier-fed rivers in the Alps and the larger rivers in Germany provide year-round training facilities which we cannot match in Britain. It is possible that the lack of big water is a major contributory factor to Britain's poorer performance on the European and World slalom circuit. However, to cope with such limitation, slalomists are taking to the mountainous rivers for

Left: *The slalom course at Augsburg was designed to produce a consistent flow of water over rocks whose shapes and exact position were computed beforehand. However the smooth artificial rocks and vertical walls produced difficult conditions. Electronic displays at each gate (the vertical boxes) gave the world instant judging decisions.*

Above: *This canoeist, having just passed through gate 9 in reverse, is already planning his tactics for the next gate. Note the diagonal line through the R and the 9 which means that the gate should not be attempted from this side.*

Left: *An East German paddler competing in an international event at Llangollen. At this level of competition, on this type of water, few competitors score high penalty points by touching gates.*

Above right: *A difficult reverse gate on this punishing and exhausting course is followed by an upstream gate (26). This paddler must therefore pass to the side of gate 26 and then paddle back up through it in the relative calm of the eddy behind the artificial rock in the middle of the picture.*

Right: *Note the flat-bladed paddle used even by this international female competitor. This shot of a grade 3 rapid shows clearly the drop in river bed levels with a flat area of water below the fall conveniently situated for collecting a group or 'flotsam'.*

Previous page: *An international C2 pair show the concentration and aggression which must be maintained throughout their run at Llangollen Town.*

their spate of winter training, while negotiation continues for more facilities such as the River Tryweryn.

An Olympic champion is analogous to the uppermost grain in a heap of sand. The position of each grain is supported by those beneath and the dimensions of the base correlate closely with the height of the apex. In other words, the growth in the numbers of slalom canoeists in Britain will inevitably raise, not only the general standards, but also the levels of skill of the competitors at the top, until eventually an Olympic champion is produced.

Of course, we in this country have enjoyed success previously in all events and our ladies are currently doing very well, but for a continuance of this trend we need a greater depth of talent. If every new competitor continues to aim high, then the intensity of competition will reward individuals and country alike.

Tough at the Top

Success in any sphere is a combination of natural talent and hard work. Many natural talents and particular physical attributes combine to produce a slalomist, but a respectable level of success is only achieved with dedicated and meaningful training. Gone are the days when a couple of

Opposite page above: *An aggressive and skillful Ken Langford reacts automatically to the forces about him and concentrates on the gate looming at his bow. Note the large holes in the crash hat which quickly drain it following a capsize.*

Opposite page below: *The techniques of this Cambridge University canoe club paddler are examined carefully by a budding slalomist on the rock. Much can be learned by watching experts in this way.*

Below: *The power shown in this shot of the Augsburg course is the outcome of undoubtedly many hard training sessions. Note the bow loop, crash hat, buoyancy aid and number, all essential features of modern competition.*

training sessions of gate practice preceded a weekend event. The international slalomist is gradually realising that in essence he is little different from the track and field athlete who trains hard for eleven months of the year, building up strength and endurance, improving his cardio-respiratory efficiency in the hope of co-ordinating it all at the time of his event.

Many will argue that there is no substitute training for an activity than the activity itself. While there is much to be said for this approach, any activity in excess can lead to a decline in motivation. To avoid this occurrence alternative training methods are to be wholly recommended provided they are constructive and well designed.

It is now becoming quite common for top class slalomists to include weight training, circuit training and some form of endurance training along with sporadic paddling and white water races during the winter months. This is the time when muscle bulk and strength is aimed for, while later in this 'off season' period they begin to concentrate on the more specific skills of gate technique and boat handling.

To ignore training is now becoming arrogant and those who rely on their experience to maintain their ranking position often find themselves placed well below their expected level. The slalom canoeist often finds the length of competition to be in the region of five to six minutes. During this period he is competing against the clock on turbulent and agitated water where an error of judgement, whether physical or perceptual, can lead to disaster. To misinterpret the speed or force of a current can lead to valuable seconds being lost or at worst a fifty seconds penalty as a gate is irretrievably missed. Therefore the pressure on those at the top is considerable. They are defending a position which many others are striving hard for and in so doing they must bring to bear the fruits of those long hard months of training with minimum errors.

A relatively new system of promotion and demotion, described later, now makes it straight-forward for a young talented canoeist to reach the higher divisions. However, this same system ensures that for him to stay there, he must maintain a fairly high level of skill, interest and training.

Components of Slalom Skills

It is not intended to quantify the psychological characteristics of the successful competitor since these will vary between individuals. Such personality traits as aggression, determination, self motivation and dedication found in the slalomist are common to most sportsmen. However, for the uninformed, a brief discussion of

the principal skill components might be useful.

In any activity where apparatus or equipment is used, it is of paramount importance to have a thorough understanding of its design characteristics. So critical is this aspect that slalom equipment is treated and discussed separately.

A study and understanding of water mechanics is a facet of slalom to which many do not pay enough attention. It is essential to know how a river works, where the main current flows and why, and what the effects are of submerged rocks or an undulating river bed on surface water patterns. It is often not apparent to novice canoeists that some areas of a river are stationary or even flow upstream.

A particular mechanical characteristic of a river which preoccupies the mind of a slalomist is its 'turning potential'. A skillful competitor will utilize the current to his advantage and will let the river do the work. For example, if a log, floating downstream is forced by the current into an area

Left: *Peter Van Stipdonk of Holland competing at the International Llangollen Slalom. Concentration coupled with precise balance is a mark of competence.*

Below: *Irish competitor Dave Talbot competing at the Monschau International Slalom. A support stroke on his right is necessary to accommodate the body lean. Compare with the photograph overleaf.*

of water that is stationary (slack water) then this will produce an effect of temporarily anchoring the front of the log while the current, acting on the remainder, turns it round. This is what is meant by turning potential. Turning potential is at its maximum where a rapid current flows adjacent to slack water and this soon becomes obvious to the novice. However, a turning potential is always present wherever there is a slight differential between adjacent currents, albeit in the same downstream direction. It is this situation which is difficult to detect quickly and then it is only apparent to the vigilant and skilled canoeist.

Therefore, not only is it important to realise that any stretch of white water forms an intricate pattern of currents moving at varying speeds in different directions, but there is a special perceptual ability of pattern recognition necessary for their utilization. Words might highlight the problem, but a conscientious and extensive study of moving water is the ultimate solution.

This C2 pair both seem to know where they should be going, but the purpose-built Olympic course with vertical walls produced often unusual and unpredictable water patterns.

A misinterpretation of the current or an inappropriate paddle stroke can lead to disaster as this competitor has discovered at Monschau in West Germany, and the apparent verbiage is of no use to him.

An understanding of current is often referred to as 'reading water' and its importance becomes much more pronounced in the higher division and on the international scene. At these slaloms free practice is prohibited and competitors must be content to study the currents and related water patterns to determine their tactics and route. It is apparent then that the competitor who can read water well and interpret its implications will be least surprised at what is in store in his first attack on the course.

A kayak to the canoeist is like a pair of skis to the skier, and as the skier wears skis, so the canoeist must wear his kayak. It is essential that for proficient boat-handling skills the canoeist must be in contact with his craft at the feet, knees and all around the seat. This is so that forces transmitted to the kayak through the arms of the canoeist from the paddle are instant and positive. Likewise there are signals from the current conveying its force and speed, which are transmitted through the canoeists' proprioceptive system to his brain, which then responds with appropriate signals. All these can be grouped together conveniently as sensory skills.

Slalom skill is not all confined to paddling a boat, a great deal is involved in reading water, deciding what is likely to happen at any particular spot and then working out your route and tactics.

The level of sensory ability in an individual, is thought to be determined at birth. Therefore the most one can do is to capitalise on the amount which is inherited and practise until one is as proficient as possible. What are we talking about here are such things as reaction time, proprioceptive feedback and balance, to mention but a few.

Most canoeists learn how to propel a kayak in many different directions very early in their career. Some may learn the Eskimo roll as their first skill, and this progression is to be recommended and applauded. However, these basic boat-handling skills are put into context on rapid rivers and it is here that an instant interpretation of the appropriate stroke, or the necessary force and the degree of body tilt, involve the sensory and perceptual components of skilled behaviour.

Divisional System

There have been several references so far to the 'divisions', so it seems appropriate now to explain its structure.

The British Canoe Union is the governing body of all types of canoeing in Britain. In 1976 The Welsh Canoeing Association was formed which caters for the Welsh canoeist, but in essence is identical and enjoys reciprocal rights with the B.C.U. Within the structure of B.C.U. there is a slalom committee which administers this aspect of the sport.

To cater for competitors of all degrees of experience, slaloms and competitors are divided into divisions similar to the football league, as follows:

1. There are four divisions for K1 men only.
2. Four divisions for K1 ladies only.

A C2 pair in practice on the Olympic course; many took the opportunity of photographing the best in the world in action.

3. Two divisions, A and B, for C1 men only.

4. Two divisions, A and B, for C2, for men and women.

All newcomers to the sport compete in Novice events and one in every five of these competitors is promoted to 4th division, i.e. a slalom with 20 competitors means that the first 4 are promoted.

Promotions from divisions 4 to division 3 are in a ratio of 1 to 10. From that division upwards to the first division one in every twenty competitors is promoted at an event.

An alternative method of promotion to an outright win is by consistently good average result over the season. The season begins in March and terminates in October and the annual results of promotion and demotion are published by the Slalom Committee after Christmas.

Slalom Equipment

Although equipment has been covered generally at the beginning of this book the more specific

Note the design of this modern (1976) slalom kayak. The dolphin-like bow shown here does little more than comply with the rules in regard to length of the boat.

items pertaining to slalom will be covered here.

1. Kayak or Canadian

a) One outstanding requirement of a slalom boat is its manoeuvrability. A competitor is constantly making rapid adjustment in one direction or another as he weaves his way through gates.

The profile from bow to stern of a highly manoeuvrable boat is banana shaped i.e., a highly-rockered keel. The cross section is dish shaped to allow sideways movement.

b) A second requirement is speed between gates, after all a competitor is being timed over the course. To achieve speed normally the profile is flatter with little rocker.

We have, therefore, a paradox. Ideally we want a highly manoeuvrable boat but at the same time we want a fast boat, so unfortunately we have to settle for a compromise. Some manufacturers have produced boats which were designed for specific international slalom courses and these have often been less effective on other rivers.

Many new boat models are similar in principle to new cars. They look different, often pleasing aesthetically, but essentially they handle in much the same way as the previous model. What the newcomer to slalom must realise is that the division 1 paddlers are not demonstrating their expertise because of the latest boats they are using, but simply because of their skill. Most of these slalomists, given a little time to familiarise themselves with a different boat, will perform equally well in it.

To the novice therefore the points to look for in choosing a boat are as follows:

Buoyancy: This is the volume of air contained in the boat. A heavy person will need a model which is more buoyant than the one required by a light person. If one sits in a boat on flat water and the side of the boat — the gunwhale — is close to the water surface then the boat is not buoyant enough. This general rule is less applicable to Canadian canoes than to kayaks.

Permanent buoyancy, for example trapped air in the form of polystyrene or buoyancy bags, should occupy as much of the boat as possible so that little water can enter in the event of a capsize.

Fit: It has already been mentioned that one *wears* a boat thus producing maximum contact between canoeist and kayak. Another essential point to note is that the footrest must be firm and a solid block of polystyrene fitted at comfortable leg

For some at Augsburg, the going was too much. Note the buoyancy provided by a) the buoyancy aid and b) the trapped air in the canoe. Help is close at hand from the two rescuers dressed in wet suits on the bank.

An early shot of a slalomist at Builth Wells, note the buoyancy aid, now legally unacceptable in slalom competition. The area of water immediately round the paddler is characteristic of grade 2-3 water.

length is much better than the foot bars which are supplied with standard new models.

Few manufacturers provide a range of seats to fit various body builds. Therefore if the seat is too wide, then attach neoprene or closed cell foam to the sides of the seat to narrow the fit.

Some competitors will order a new boat devoid of fittings so they can attach their own. Many will fit additional knee bars to increase security. A great fear of many novice canoeists is that these close fitting boats will not allow escape in emergency. On the contrary it is most difficult to stay in these canoes once they are capsized. The water acts as a lubricant and the canoeist frequently finds himself sliding out, much to his annoyance, as he attempts his much practised Eskimo roll.

2. Buoyancy aid or lifejacket

Whichever is chosen the rules state that there must be minimum buoyancy of 6 kg. The lifejacket is designed to turn an immersed victim onto his back, thus allowing him maximum ventilation. However, these garments are not favoured extensively by slalomists due largely to their bulkiness. Buoyancy aids, seen extensively in the illustrations, come in many colours with or without front zips. Not only do they provide buoyancy but they are quite effective windproofs.

3. Crash hats

A variety of designs, some with chin guards some without, all incorporate holes to allow water to escape following immersion. The purpose, obviously, is to protect the head but not always from the rocks encountered during a capsize, more frequently from swinging poles on the course.

4. Paddles

Curved blades are more efficient than flat blades and an oval loom automatically indicates to the paddler the orientation of his blade without him looking at it. The correct length depends on anatomical height but a rough guide is for the paddler to be able to grip the top of the vertical paddle, while standing.

5. Bow and stern loops

A loop of cord at the bow and stern is essential. A refined attachment is a toggle or small plastic ball which is much more comfortable to hold when swimming with the boat. These you will rarely see on the craft of skilled slalomists for two reasons. First protrusions, such as these, occasionally cause penalty points as they pass between gates. Second and more important the principle of bow and stern attachments is that of safety i.e. holding onto the boat following capsize and abandonment, but to the skilled canoeist a capsize is corrected by a roll, not a swim ashore. Far from being an arrogant statement it is mere fact that to be able to roll proficiently means without fail in all conditions. To take this issue a step further of course, some might argue that the aim and skill in canoeing is to keep the craft upright. Therefore, although one must have bow and stern loops, aim to avoid having to use them because of your failsafe rolling skills.

Cost

It would be unwise and immediately out of date to give specific figures for the cost of equipment. Compared with another outdoor sport such as mountaineering, the cost of a kayak (1977) is only 30 per cent more than a good pair of boots, and the total cost of a paddle, crash hat, and buoyancy aid is approximately 50 per cent of a pair of boots.

A list of manufacturers, who will be pleased to supply current prices, is given in the appendix.

Transport

As with many outdoor pursuits, transport for a competitor and his equipment to the event is essential. However, it can still be reasonably economical by sharing transport and costs with others. This is one of the main advantages of joining a club where one mini bus and trailer can cater for more than a dozen competitors.

How to Start

Interest in slalom may have resulted from reading about, hearing about or seeing the sport. Whichever the origin, it is wise to 'have a go' before committing yourself to expensive equipment. The most obvious method is to approach a club and express your interest and eagerness to try slalom. Most clubs will be more than willing to help you to develop your interest and will give you informed guidance on the choice of equipment.

Many clubs own a pool of equipment which is available for their novice members to use. They organize local training events which may range from swimming pool rolling sessions, local races or slaloms, to surf championships. Many of the larger clubs organize national ranking slaloms and international events. The many advantages of joining a club have been mentioned elsewhere in this book and it need only be reiterated that this is undoubtedly the best way of being introduced to canoeing, particularly slalom.

Joining a club, however, is not the only way, and indeed many individuals may discover that a local club does not exist and the nearest is an unreasonable distance away. What in fact is a club? Is it not simply a group of individuals with a common interest who occasionally meet together to talk about and practice their sport? There is no necessity for a club house, a chairman or club fees; these develop later as the group grows in size. To start canoeing as a novice therefore, you need to find another canoeist, or better still, a slalomist with whom you can visit slaloms, first as a spectator, then as a competitor. To find another local canoeist is not always easy but in such cases a request to the General Secretary of the British Canoe Union for the address (Appendix 1) of the local coaching organiser will be worthwhile. Britain is divided into canoeing areas, each of which is allocated to a person responsible for co-ordinating, developing and administering canoeing (coaching). This person has a list of active canoeists in his area and will be most willing to inform you of their whereabouts.

Age

Canoeing is for all age groups and slalom particularly caters for those from ten to sixty years old. If you wish to extend this age range, at either end, then feel free to join us and enjoy the thrills and spills of a sport which caters for all abilities.

Surf Canoeing

Most of the canoeists we know look upon surfing as a fun activity. At basic level one achieves maximum sport with perhaps minimum skill compared to other white water aspects of canoeing. This does not imply that skillful performance is rapidly achieved.

Board surfing is literally centuries old: evidence indicates that the natives of Hawaii cavorted in the sea on what can only be described as surf boards. Canoe surfing, although tried to some extent in the days of the heavy Victorian kayaks, and later in the canvas craft of the early Fifties, has progressed since the advent of glassfibre construction which lead to the boom of the last ten years. We can recall many days spent on the surf around the Snowdonia National Park when there were no other boats other than those of our party and it was only during holidays that the clubs from Manchester, Chester, Leeds and Birmingham came down.

One met and shared waves with many of the slalom personalities and it was such a natural outlet that it complemented river sport. The kayaks used were invariably slalom boats which had been battered and thus relegated to surfing. The sea bashed them to final destruction.

Much has already been said about equipment, indeed we have re-iterated several points deliberately. In surfing we would like you to consider how to counteract the force of the waves. One of our own students emerged from the sea at Porth Ceiriad on Lleyn, wearing the deck of his kayak, unaware and not particularly caring where the hull had got to!

Joints between components of the boat must be reinforced and must be well supported vertically to withstand the weight of water on the deck. Polystyrene block is the general method by which this is achieved but the blocks need to be held in place or they tend to work loose and can float away if you capsize.

These blocks are usually four inches to five inches in thickness and they extend from as close to the nose of the kayak as possible to as close to the foot rest as you can make them. Some canoeists actually press their foot rest into the block when first fitting it. As you grow, you can always slice off a bit of polystyrene!

The footrest itself can either be a 'Failsafe' type which will return towards the cockpit should you have the misfortune to slip past it, or, and this is what we prefer, a reinforcement of the bar into a platform and a fitting of 7/16" brass bolts in place of the average fittings. When supported by the polystyrene block the platform is very solid. One also finds that the platform is more comfortable in use. If you look at any of the action shots showing the vertical position of the paddler it does not take much imagination to appreciate fully the safety factors implicit in this advice.

The polystyrene blocks also serve as buoyancy. It is not a question of 'will one get wet' but of 'how often and to what extent?' If the buoyancy shifts then you can watch your boat sink. As a beginner, even if you have learned to roll effectively, you can expect to be caught out at some time very early in your activity. A kayak full of water is not only heavy, but potentially dangerous to yourself and other water users. Many canoeists use inflatable, shaped buoyancy bags and they are fine in the stern. The bow half can be filled with car inner tubes, forced in between the block and the gunwhales, empty sherry containers, which many wine shops will be happy to give you, or even one gallon squash containers. The remarks about holding them firm are still relevant. The fuller the kayak is of semi flexible, inflatable buoyancy, the less sea space there is to create a considerable, heavy problem when you capsize and have to swim into shore. By the same token, if you hang on to your boat, it will serve as a buoyancy aid and identify you. If you leave your boat at sea, just consider that a small head — yours — is less likely to be spotted than fifteen feet of coloured plastic.

Spray decks need to fit tightly. Some people use two, one on top of the other, for extra support against the falling wave. Even if you think you can roll, a toggle to lift the spray cover can be useful, especially if your hands are cold.

Similarly, as mentioned before, toggles made

Above: *'You must be able to roll effectively.'* Below: *Spray decks must fit tightly.*

Emptying a surf shoe. Note the toggle fixed to the bow.

Two modern surf kayaks, showing deck fittings and hull shapes. Note the ladder type of roof rack.

from about four inches of broom handle and threaded to a piece of five-millimetre nylon cord are better than loops in surf. The kayak can rotate in the waves and tighten a loop up on your hand, whereas the toggle is easier to grab and hold. Check the condition of these loops regularly.

Choice of paddles is pretty simple: any slalom blades will do and many good surfers still use the big, flat 'Manchester' paddles. The round loomed paddles are not ideal but they may be easily modified by squeezing the loom in a woodworkers vice to oval them, making sure that the ovality suits the grip relative to the flat of the blade.

So much for the boat and paddles. We have already advised about dress, personal buoyancy aid and crash hats. Similarly we have noted the need to be warm yet to preserve freedom in colder months by wearing wool next to the skin covered by either a dry suit top or a good canoe anorak.

The more recent development of surf canoeing and surf competition has been the surf 'shoe' as the early specialist boats were called. Many of the photographs show these short, flat-bottomed kayaks to great effect.

They are designed to be closely similar to the surf board. They have good running potential and a manoeuvrability quite different from a slalom

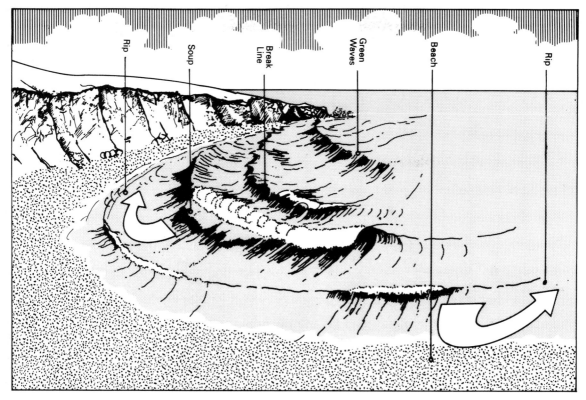

Above: *Surf beaches and rips* Below: *Profile*

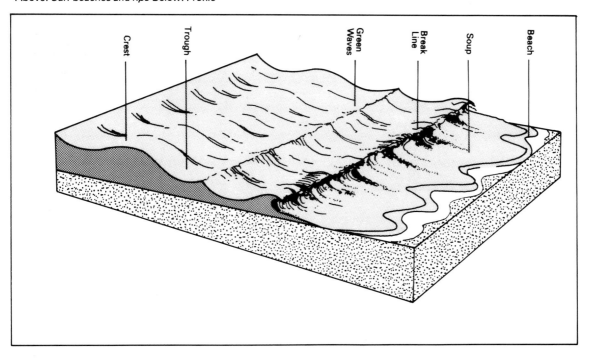

Keep a sharp eye out for other surf users around you.

kayak. The surf kayak 'slips' on the face of a wave unless the occupant angles the inside edge into the wave and holds a line. This is similar to skiing on snow in principle. When the canoeist deliberately flattens the craft it can slip and with skill, be rotated on the face of the wave through a 360 degree turn.

All the factors of buoyancy, fit, etc. apply to the special surf kayak.

At this moment, designers are working on an unsinkable surf ski-kayak. This is like a surf board with a seat-cum-leg grip arrangement which allows the paddler to roll as one would in a kayak. This development has stemmed from a need experienced in rescue work. There is less to go wrong and the skills of the canoeist are directly transferable. It has yet to be seen as a fun boat but who knows?

Let us now look at a typical surf beach. To begin with, we advise that you find a small, enclosed beach rather than a large, often windswept one. Always go surfing with at least one other person: surfing in big waves is no place for a loner and shore support should be capable of making a positive contribution, not just being there to help you empty out and shout. Perhaps the best thing to do to encourage a parent is to persuade him, her, or both, that it is a good sport for them; many

parents of teenagers are still very good paddlers.

We have just said 'Let us look at a surf beach'. Do just that. Every beach has its own idiosyncrasies, rocks, inlets of river or small stream and currents. The sea bed creates many of the currents and may break, slow down or speed up the wave motion. Climb to a high vantage point and study carefully what is happening on the sea surface. Five minutes is just not sufficient time, quarter of an hour is more realistic, and look for the signs which in particular indicate the rip currents.

The rips are points at which the water runs back out to sea. Obvious ones will flow strongly, but look for flotsam which is being held or is moving outwards and the flow will become more easily apparent. Rip currents are at their strongest as the tide flows in. They also occur at the outflow of streams.

The effect of a rip current, apart from its counter-flow, is that incoming waves are flattened out. This flattening gives the surfer a safe means of getting through the 'break line' to the green waves beyond. Since the effect is constant, there will be no board riders or other paddlers boring in as you paddle out.

If paddlers can, by tacit understanding, stick to the pattern of the currents then the basis of good

These canoeists are sharing a wave. For a novice, this would be too close a situation for safety.

discipline is formed. The 'run in' area is clear and a circular chain of activity is established.

Discipline is perhaps first appreciated when one considers the other users of the surf, particularly swimmers and board surfers.

Swimmers rarely understand or anticipate the speed attained by a kayak on surf, nor the hardness of fibreglass. On some popular surf beaches there is an attempt to 'zone'. Swimmers and surfers are often allocated areas of beach, and persuaded by lifeguards and flags to stick to their zone. However, a swimmer may be present in the canoeing zone in the form of a capsized canoeist or board surfer. Keep your eyes open and keep them 'roving': consider that a swimmer could be in a wave trough on leaving a water logged kayak in the 'soup'. Give swimmers space and consideration. This is even more essential when you try reverse skills.

The ultimate in self discipline is when a collision between boats seems inevitable. Both canoeists must capsize. The effect of the body under water is to anchor the unit and the wave passes the upturned craft. Experienced canoeists will auto-matically respond to this need, allow a few seconds before rolling up, then survey the scene afresh.

Finally if a paddler is in trouble only the experienced canoeist should attempt to rescue him or his boat. The rescue can be equally effective by drawing the attention of others to someone in difficulty, or if he is beyond the surf line by staying with the victim. In big waves, the force of water may cause the owner to lose his boat; if possible accompany the swimmer to safety, disembark and together you are in a stronger position to retrieve the craft and empty it. A selfish surf canoeist should not exist.

Looking at the action pictures will impress upon you that there is a repertoire of activity appropriate to the two classes of surf kayak. Before studying this area of performance, one needs to understand wave form and its passage from the first, green swell to foaming, air-filled soup and the beach.

In the U.K. the prevailing winds are the South Westerlies. The largest, uninterrupted stretch of water approaching our shores is the Atlantic

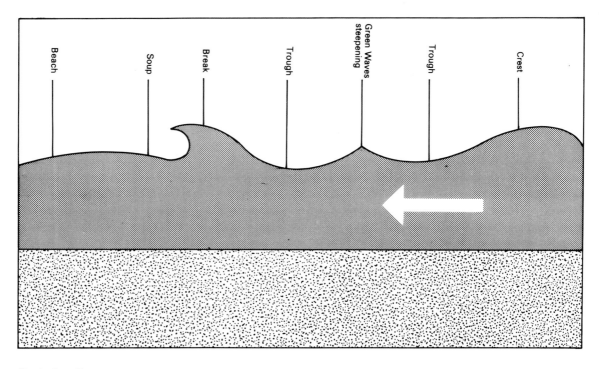

Beach

Soup

Break

Trough

Green Waves
steepening

Trough

Crest

Sea bed profile

Ocean. Waves from the ocean hit the south-west coast without losing momentum and they are assisted, more often than not, by the prevailing wind. Upon these factors is based the opinion that the best consistent surf in Britain occurs in Cornwall and South-West Devon. From Bude Bay to Sennen one can find good surf.

The angle at which the sea bed shelves towards the land is a factor which affects the shape and speed of waves. Steeply inclined beaches tend to give steep waves but of relatively short running potential. Conversely, a shallow gradient tends to produce green waves of less steep profile, giving long runs but less scope for acrobatics.

Fortunately, good surf is not confined to the south west. The width of the Irish Sea provides sufficient 'fetch' to give good and often excellent surf throughout Wales, helped by the same winds. Scotland is being explored and some pioneers rave about conditions to the west of the Highlands. Occasionally, the North-East winds give support to the East coast but the tendency is in favour of the West.

For the keen traveller both France and Ireland offer good surf venues, detail of which can be obtained via the larger clubs or the B.C.U.

Balance is the crux of the issue in relation to surf technique. Paddle out at ninety degrees towards

the incoming waves and stop before the break line. Paddle around in the white foaming soup between the break and the shore and feel the pushing action of water against the kayak hull. You will soon learn that if you lean your kayak towards the beach, the smallest wave or turbulence will capsize you. If you incline the hull into the oncoming wave, preferably with a hip movement rather than a full body lean, as in the diagram above right, you will be pushed sideways towards the shore. The paddle is held in a support position on small soup but in larger soup and on the break as in the photograph to the right the 'high brace' is correct and is a stronger position. There is no quick solution in this sport: only practice on the water will build up skill. The ability to roll, which in surf is often wave-assisted, is most desirable and ultimately essential. Reach for the point at which you can ride in, using hip movement and balance only and the paddle can be lifted from the surface of the sea.

Once you have become accustomed to the feel of the soup, attempt to catch the wave and ride in on it. First paddle before the wave reaches you, let it catch you, lift the stern and propel you shorewards. What happens next is that you will turn or be turned. If you turn by paddling and leaning, as on a river, you will end up with a brace

56

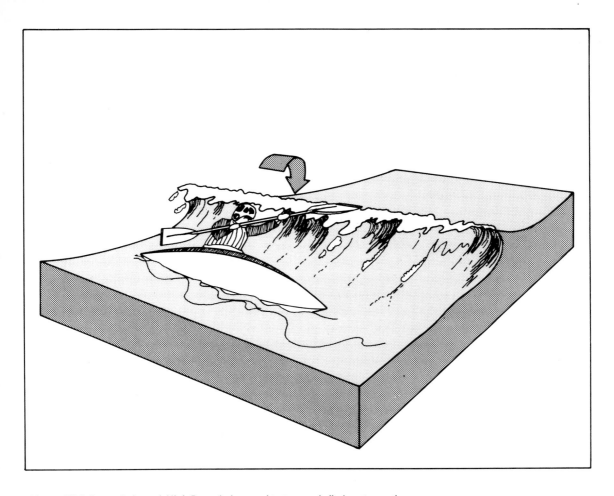

Above: *High Brace.* Below: *A High Brace being used to turn and climb out over the wave.*

Above: *Turning from Telemark to High Brace in a slalom kayak.* Below: *Correct and incorrect position needed to catch a chosen wave successfully.*

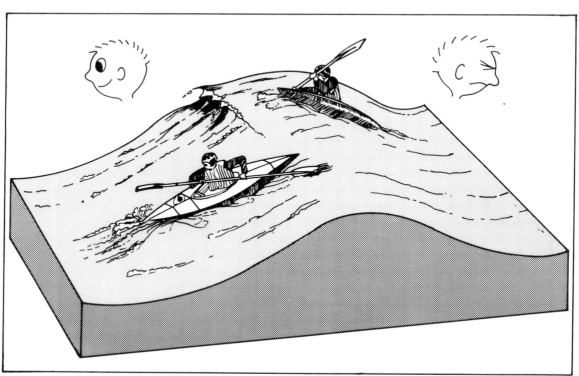

Above: *Missing the wave.* Below: *Catching the wave. Note the stern rudder in use.*

Above and facing: *'To judge the shoulder and then ride just in front of the break, to pull out and over the top before becoming engulfed is what a good surf run is about.'*

position and moving sideways. If turned, you must anticipate quickly the direction to lean and brace before the wave tips you in. You must expect constant capsizes at this stage.

In most of the photographs showing running action, you can see that the paddle is used as a stern rudder. On long runs the rudder is held firmly on the down wave side of the boat. The effect produced is to hold course. If one wishes to ride and not to become airborne in the break of the wave, then the canoeist shifts the down wave rudder to the telemark position, inclines the boat into the intended turn and climbs back, at speed, up the wave to paddle out to sea again. Before one starts a run however, the canoeist has to choose, then 'catch' his wave.

Waves tend to arrive in 'sets' which geneally increase in height throughout the sequence. If in a group, it is wise to stagger the action. A paddler who finds himself well positioned will often shout 'Mine' before making the three or four vigorous strokes needed to place his craft onto the wave face. At this point you are on the downhill running position. As in the two photographs on the previous page and in the sketch, you will see that if your take off lacks force, or is timed too late, you will fall behind the wave and miss your ride.

We have now reached the point when we can consider the types of run available. The longest and fastest run occurs with the boat set at an angle — this is obvious when you realize that the diagonal line is longer than the direct one — but as you travel at the speed of the wave, so you have to cover more distance in the same time span.

If you study the manner and the point of commencement of the break, you may observe what is known as a shoulder. This is seen clearly in the photographs. To judge the shoulder and then ride just in front of the break, to pull out and over the top before becoming engulfed, is what a good surf run is about.

Unfortunately, shoulders only occur when

conditions are favourable. The wind may flatten waves or the break may start from one or more points. In this instance one may constantly swing from left to right to maintain a run before pulling out quickly from convergent shoulder breaks. This is shown in the photograph below.

The specialist surf kayak is more responsive than the slalom boat but the reading of the wave and handling skills are basically similar.

Running straight down a wave at ninety degrees to the line of it, will, on small waves or less steep ones, give you a good run. Sooner or later, by accident rather than by choice, one wave will

steepen behind you and the nose of your boat will dig into water or sand. You will be airborne and wonder what on earth has happened. Once recovered, you will want to repeat the experience. The following section explains the basic repertoire of surf acrobatics.

The 'dip' or 'pop out' is the simplest skill and is the starting point of all the others. The line of the boat must be a true ninety degrees to the line of the wave in order that the kayak lifts squarely. You achieve this position by rapid and effective use of the stern rudder and hips. Once the bow burrows into the water the wave face advances, lifting the

If a break starts from one or more points one may constantly swing from left to right to maintain a run before pulling out quickly from converging shoulder breaks.

Above: *A fine study of the down wave stern rudder position.* Below: *There is no way out for this man except a quick climb up and over the top before the full break catches him.*

The starting position for all kayak acrobatics. Note the high, vertical position. This man will loop since his body has moved forwards.

The movement continues. The paddler has already anticipated his roll by placing his paddle to the side nearest the camera.

This shot shows how, from the vertical, the canoeist has leaned back and shows the distinctive twisting action of his body. He has already used his paddle which aids his rotation.

craft to the vertical. At this point, the occupant leans back. The wave passes the kayak which then falls back, on even keel behind the wave.

The first refinement, known as a 'sky rocket', is when the paddler chooses a very steep wave, close to the point of breaking so that he starts the manoeuvre from as high up the wave face as possible. The kayak then accelerates down the wave with great force and the reaction squeezes the boat like a pip and it is not abnormal to be completely free of the water, hence the name 'sky rocket'.

The 'forward loop' is achieved from the same vertical position, the difference being that the canoeist deliberately leans forwards, towards the bow. This directional placement of weight continues the line of momentum and the kayak will either fall over or lift and fall forwards. The paddler rolls and if he is capable of a fast recovery, may stay on the same wave. On a wave which reforms itself the performer may obtain two thrills from one wave.

The photographs above and right, show how, from the vertical, uplifted position, the paddler, by

66

This man is using a back-paddle stroke with body twist to achieve this spin out. Note in particular how close the body is lying to the kayak rear deck.

The flat hull form allows for rotation and gives flat, sliding contact with the wave.

means of a combined leg-hip twisting movement and paddle stroke, may pirouette. The object of this skill is to remain upright, facing out to sea.

Split-second timing comes only from hours of practice and this skill is applicable to the slalom rather than the surf kayak. However, one can only stress that these performances stem from correct, vertical positioning which itself is linked to good and quick use of stern rudder, hip adjustment and that final component, balance.

Special surf kayaks lend themselves to greater facility in reverse manoeuvres due to the low level of the rear of the cockpit. The basic positioning is that described for forward skills with the slalom boat.

Additionally, as already stated, the flat hull form allows for rotation and the photographs show stages in this process. The difference between the flat, sliding contact with the wave is shown in the photograph above and contrasts with the photograph above right where the angle of the edge of the hull is clearly driving the surface back up and over the face of the wave.

These skills are still being developed, so perhaps the younger surf canoeist reading this book will be the next trendsetter in this exciting aspect of the sport.

Above: *The angle-edged hull form can clearly be seen driving the surfer back up and over the face of the wave.*
Below: *Leaning into a turn. This man will probably end up in a 'side on' position.*

Two side slipping shots. Note the flat hulls pushing water towards the camera.

Left: *This photograph epitomises surf sport: Speed, spray and action are all evident.*

One final word is due concerning the effect of an off-shore wind. If the surf is good then the waves tend to be held up and steepened by an off-shore wind. This produces a sudden break which is called a 'dumping wave': the water drops rather than flows and if a canoeist is caught sideways on, then his boat must withstand tremendous pressure and weight. The novice should be very careful in such conditions. For the expert, dumpers are synonymous with the ultimate in kayak acrobatics but they rarely give long rides or rotational prospects for the specialist, modern craft.

Surf canoeing is an all season sport. It is thrilling but because of high speed and big water it is potentially hazardous. Being a good performer does not necessarily mean that one is a responsible surf canoeist; you should aim to be both.

Tired and happy: carrying a surf kayak out of the sea after a good, hard day.

Interview

To conclude this book we visited St. Davids Boarding School at Llandudno and met a group of boys from the school's very active canoe club. These boys were given the opportunity to ask questions about any aspect of canoeing and to receive answers from the authors as an addition to their own teachers who were also present. In the following pages we present their questions, which hopefully are typical novice enquiries. Many questions, of course, have been pre-empted in the preparation of this book and where a more complete answer is stated elsewhere this is indicated.

Q. 1 Which type of boat would you recommend for slalom?

A. 1 (Refer slalom equipment). We would advise you to look at the characteristics of boat design and to link these with your own body build. Designs with a lot of rocker are highly manoeuvrable, those with little rocker are more suited to speed. In a slalom you need a highly manoeuvrable boat within gates but a fast boat between gates so the best you can hope for is a balance between these two characteristics. A heavy person will perform better in a more buoyant boat than in a lowline type: but a light person is in a position to consider a less buoyant craft.

Q. 2 What sort of boat do you recommend for slalom, white water, touring and surfing?

A. 2 (Refer white water and surf equipment). We feel that a general purpose, glassfibre slalom kayak is the most appropriate. Of course, a boat being used in surf needs strengthening with extra buoyancy between deck and hull.

Q. 3 What sort of boat do you recommend for club usage?

A. 3 This has been answered largely by the previous question. One might add that a build-it-yourself glassfibre kayak undoubtedly saves you a great deal of money, in addition to giving you a positive opportunity of working with fibreglass.

Q. 4 What is the position about access?

A. 4 The situation as it stands at present is that you must obtain permission from the land owner in order to pass over his land. Hopefully this permission might be easier to secure in the future. This rule does not apply to tidal water; between high and low water mark is Crown Property.

Q. 5 Is there an upper age limit for competing in slalom?

A. 5 No, but there is an upper limit which is categorized within the 'Youth' section, which terminates on the competitor's nineteenth birthday.

Q. 6 Which strokes are necessary for surf, slalom, white water and touring?

A. 6 Strokes such as the draw and sculling are in our opinion useful in giving the novice an opportunity of getting used to his boat. They assume less significance as pure strokes in the context of moving water, where combination strokes are more appropriate. Once a novice has familiarised himself with his boat, then is the time for him to learn how to read water and how best to benefit from its power. Not enough attention is given to this latter point.

Q. 7 Do you need a wet suit?

A. 7 A wet suit serves many purposes. Wet-suit trousers or a Long John not only keep the wearer warm, but also protect him from abrasion from within the boat. A wet-suit top also keeps one warm but it can produce nasty sores around the arm and chest area. A wet suit is more efficient in water. It also gives a great deal of buoyancy.

The cost is also a major factor. For cold canoeing, with no cost constraints, wet-suit trousers or a Long John coupled with either a drysuit top or cagjak worn with woollen underwear make a good combination. A pair of wet-suit bootees are very comfortable.

Q. 8 What do I look for in a slalom paddle?

A. 8 Initially ensure correct length. Stand and raise your hand; if you can grasp the top of the paddle blade then the length is about right. If cost is a major factor then consider flat blades and a plastic covered metal loom. The next step up is to consider curved glassfibre blades with a wooden, oval loom. Undoubtedly the best design of paddle currently available is the oval wooden loom with a curved laminated wooden blade. (Refer equipment).

Q. 9 What is the best life jacket and buoyancy aid?

A. 9 (Refer equipment). A deflated lifejacket is only a buoyancy aid but to an immersed victim, who might either be able to inflate it himself, or to get a helper to do it for him, is much appreciated. On the other hand, a buoyancy aid not only keeps you afloat and keeps you warm, but it can protect your body against severe knocks. (See equipment).

Q. 10 Is it worth padding the sides of a seat?

A. 10 If you do not fit the seat snugly, then by all means pad it. If someone lifted you from the surface of the water, ideally your kayak should remain with you because of the fit. Such a fit facilitates maximum performance.

Q. 11 Where does rolling fit into a progression of skills?

A. 11 If you are lucky enough to have access to a swimming pool then there is no reason why rolling should not be the first skill on the programme. Not only is it important to be able to roll, but equally a determination to remain in the boat and roll, no matter how many attempts it might take, is the recommended attitude.

Q. 12 How can I enter a slalom?

A. 12 If you belong to a canoe club, advice of this nature is readily available to you. As an individual you must join the B.C.U. If you indicate to them that your interests lie in this direction, then you will be sent a slalom year book. In this book you will find a calendar of all slalom events, the names and addresses of the organising clubs and the secretaries to whom you send your entry and fees. In other words, absolutely everything you might want to know about slalom organisation is found in the year book.

Q. 13 Which type of crash hat do you recommend?

A. 13 Practically all of those marketed professionally are good value. Important features to look for include an adjustable band for various head sizes and a good chin strap of either nylon or leather, with a solid fastening device. To test this, fasten the buckle and apply a considerable force across this. A good design will stay closed, a poor one might slip or open easily.

An alternative is to convert an old climbing helmet or motor cycle 'skid lid' by drilling large holes in it to let out the water following a capsize.

Q. 14 How serious is the problem of head protection in shallow water?

A. 14 Water provides a considerable cushioning effect on all but sharp and pointed rocks. In shallow water you can often push off the bottom to right yourself so rolling in that particular instance is less applicable. The crash hat is also important however offering protection from passing branches or swinging slalom poles.

Q. 15 Do you need to strengthen your boat in surf?

A. 15 If your boat is to be used exclusively for surfing then you are less concerned about its weight and so more strengthening in the form of extra seams is worthwhile. However, if your boat is to be used for activities other than surfing, extra support of a secure but temporary nature must be incorporated. This can often take the form of buoyancy of an inflatable type where the internal pressure will resist the crushing effects of the waves. (See surf section).

Q. 16 How much strength is there in Gel coat?

A. 16 In a word, none. Many boat builders in the past have produced boats with thick layers of Gel coat under the mistaken impression that these are stronger. Modern manufacturers no longer do this and in fact the gel is very thin and merely serves the purpose of waterproofing the composite. Strength comes from the arrangement of the fibres within hardened resin. Resin alone has no inherent strength, so having built your boat, with 250 grams of resin to spare, do not spread this inside your hull under the mistaken impression that you are increasing its strength. You are merely increasing the weight. The order of difficulty in fibreglass boat building is as follows:
1. Very difficult — requiring care and skill — strong lightweight boat.
2. Reasonably straight forward — with care — strong but heavy boat.
3. Easy — little skill — weak and heavy boat because there is too much resin in relation to the quantity of glassfibre. An ideal proportion is seventy per cent glassfibre : thirty per cent resin.

The Authors were pleased to answer these questions, not only because they represent a cross section of those from novices at large, but also because they served to highlight the void in general knowledge about equipment. Perhaps more informative literature from the leading manufacturers might help in this area.

In addition to the above, our discussion with this group touched on the topic of training for a sport. It was encouraging to learn that relative novices such as these, with an average age of fifteen, accepted the need to train in order to achieve pleasure and competitive success, realising the immense value of activities such as running, cycling and swimming to produce general fitness.

There will of course be questions which we have not managed to answer either here or in other parts of the book but we have at least attempted to set the scene and to plant the seed of canoeing. It is now *your* task to act and to develop from here.

Appendix 1

Structure of the British Canoe Union

The British Canoe Union is recognised by the Sports Council as the governing body for the sport of canoeing in Great Britain, representing it at home and abroad. The B.C.U. is affiliated to the International Canoe Federation. The object of the B.C.U. is to promote the sport of canoeing in all its forms.

The general administration of the B.C.U. is in the hands of the Director with an office at the Sports Council Headquarters, 70 Brompton Road, London, SW3 1DT. The Director is responsible for:

Key Objectives

1. To direct the activities of the Secretariat in such a way that the objectives of the B.C.U. are met as effectively as possible, taking account of the available resources.
2. To promote the aims and policies of the B.C.U.

Responsibilities

1. As Chief Executive of the Secretariat, the Director is responsible for all its activities and directly or indirectly for the management of all its staff. He is responsible to the Executive Committee of the Council for management of the Secretariat and to the Council for achieving the objectives of the B.C.U. and carrying out policies laid down for him.
2. While delegating authority as far as possible to Departmental Managers he takes particular responsibility for the following functions:

Representation: The B.C.U. represents the canoeist's view point on a wide variety of outside committees. The Council of the B.C.U. will determine representation on such committees and may require the Director or his staff to represent it on them. It is important that this representation be diplomatic and effective.
a) Major negotiations with new sponsors.
b) Public Relations and Press Conferences (in conjunction with the Promotions Manager and Field Development Manager when appointed).

Membership of the B.C.U. is open to organisations within the British Isles and to men, women and young people of any nationality who are interested in canoeing. The organisation for clubs within the British Isles is such that those in England and Wales work direct with the headquarters whilst those in Scotland and Northern Ireland work within a local canoeing authority known as a Division. Individuals wherever they may be can correspond with and will receive their magazine and literature direct from the headquarters.

The B.C.U. is governed by a Council consisting of:
the President, the Chairman, the Hon. Treasurer, 10 elected members, 2 members nominated by each of the Divisions and 8 members nominated by the technical committees.

Although the full council has over-riding authority in all matters, it generally delegates its authority to two standing committees, formed from its own members, namely:
(a) The competition committee and
(b) The towing and access committee.
It further delegates its authority for the day to day conduct of its affairs to technical committees who are authorised to act in all matters connected with their own form of the sport. These technical committees are:
(a) Long distance racing
(b) Sprint racing
(c) Sailing racing
(d) Slalom and whitewater racing
(e) Touring
(f) Coaching and related matters
(g) Corps of Canoe Life-Guards
(h) Canoe Polo
The Coaching Committee consists of not more than one representative from each of the other technical committees, the area coaching organisers, and a representative of the Sports Council. The Coaching Scheme is administered by the Director of Coaching.

Every club affiliated to the B.C.U. is entitled to have two representatives on each of these technical committees, except the Coaching committee. Such representatives must be full members. It is clear that if every affiliated club exercised its right to nominate two members for each committee the size of the committees would be such that they would be quite unmanageable. In practice, clubs only nominate members to the technical committees in which they are particularly interested. These technical committees elect their own Chairman and Secretary and decide on their own procedure. However the decisions of the committees on matters of principle must be submitted to the Council or to one of the Council's standing committees dealing with the particular subject.

Following upon the setting up of a Sports Council it has been necessary to nominate B.C.U. representatives to each of the regional sports conferences or associations who elect the sports representatives to the appropriate regional Sports Council. Many counties have also formed sports associations and B.C.U. representatives have been nominated for each county so that canoeing shall be represented at all such meetings. B.C.U. county representatives are expected to obtain information from B.C.U. affiliated clubs in their areas, and in addition to make representations on county sports matters to keep the B.C.U. regional sports representative informed so that action may be taken in regional Sports Councils.

General guidance to regional and county representatives is given by the B.C.U. Council.

B.C.U. Membership

There are three types of membership.

Individual Members
a) Full Membership. There is no entrance fee.
b) Youth Membership. Those who have not reached their 19th birthday by the 1st January may, if they wish, become Youth Members. Youth Members have all the privileges of Full Members except voting rights and the right to sit on Technical Committees.
c) Family Membership. Provided that at least one member of a family joins as a Full Member, other members of a family may become Family Members by paying an annual subscription, regardless of age. Family Members have all the privileges of a Full Member, except voting rights, the right to sit on Technical Committees and they do not receive individual copies of the magazine or any other general communications.

Privileges Offered to Individual Members: B.C.U. individual members have the right to obtain advice and information on Canoe Touring at home and abroad and all other canoeing matters. They also have the right to take part in B.C.U. sponsored or recognised events.

B.C.U. members may purchase publications and film loops at preferential rates and items from the stocks of maps, guides and canoeing books. They can take B.C.U. tests at preferential rates.

B.C.U. members have the right to take part in the management of its affairs; to wear its badges and tie and to fly its pennant; they receive the B.C.U. magazine free. The B.C.U. has negotiated a members' Canoe Insurance and can offer its members cover at very low rates.

Affiliated Members
Affiliation is open to any canoeing body in the United Kingdom. Service Unit Canoe Clubs stationed overseas may also affiliate. Also Canoe Clubs, Schools' and Youth Canoeing Associations, canoeing sections of other bodies, etc.

Privileges Offered to Affiliated Bodies: The right to seek recognition of its canoeing events; the right to purchase certain goods and to obtain certain services at preferential prices; the right to seek to recruit unattached Individual Members of the B.C.U. and provided that at least ten of its members are Full Individual Members of the B.C.U.; the right to nominate two of those members to each of the Technical Committees and the further right to a voice and a vote at General Meetings of the B.C.U.

The members of an affiliated body derive no personal privileges from their organisation's membership of the B.C.U. Bodies seeking affiliation promise to do all they can to encourage their own members to join the B.C.U.

Affiliated bodies agree to be bound by the Rules and Regulations of the B.C.U. whether or not they themselves are members. Each of the Technical Committees is empowered to draft regulations affecting its own aspect of the sport.

Associates
These are organisations with an interest in canoeing and who wish to support the objects of the Union. Associateship is open to any non-canoeing body who wishes to have contact with the B.C.U., e.g. Local Education Authorities. Associates have no voting rights but may seek advice and will receive canoeing news from time to time.

N.B. The B.C.U.'s financial year is from 1st November to 31st October. Those who join between 1st September and 31st October are members until 31st October of the following year.

Open Affiliated Clubs

The following is a selection of clubs with their addresses who encourage young canoeists.

London and South East (Greater London, Middlesex, Kent, Surrey, Sussex)

Isleworth Canoe Club:
c/o K. N. East, 35 Almorah Road, Heston, Middlesex.
Royal Canoe Club:
c/o Mrs. G. V. Barnard, Clubhouse, Trowlock Island, Teddington, Middlesex.
Shoreham Kayak Club:
c/o Mrs. P. A. Newman, 74 West Way, Hove, Sussex, BN3 8LR.

South (Berkshire, Buckinghamshire, Hampshire, Isle of Wight, Oxfordshire)
Calshot Activities Centre:
c/o G. C. Good, Calshot Spit, Calshot, Southampton, Hants.
Chalfont Park Canoe Club:
c/o Malcolm Box, 68 Franklin Road, London NW 10.
Reading Kayak Club:
c/o Peter Brothers, Flat 12, Southcote Manor, 186 Hertford Road, Southcote, Reading, Berks.
Reading & Leighton Park Canoe Club:
c/o B. Perrett, 4 South Drive, Leighton Park School, Reading, Berks.
Riverside Canoe Club:
c/o The Warden, Riverside Centre, Donnington Bridge, Oxford.
Sinodum Youth & Community Committee:
c/o A. H. Taylor, 55 High Street, Wallingford, Oxon. OX10 0DB.
Warren Canoe Club:
c/o Canoeing Organiser, Central Club, 29 Chain Street, Reading, Berks.
Windsor & District Canoe Club:
c/o D. C. Hedges, 18 Arlington Rd., Ashford, Middx.

South West (Avon, Cornwall, Devon, Dorset, Gloucestershire, Somerset, Wiltshire).
Bristol Canoe Club:
c/o Alan Williams, 17 Philippa Close, Whitchurch, Bristol, Avon.
St. Austell Canoe Club:
c/o J. C. Kuyser, Kozee Mott, Menear Road, St. Austell, Cornwall.

East (Bedfordshire, Cambridgeshire, Essex, Hertfordshire, Norfolk, Suffolk)
Norfolk Canoeing Association:
c/o The Secretary, 104 Orchard Close, Thorpe, Norwich, NOR 0SR.
Sele Y C Canoe Club:
c/o P. Breckon, The Sele School, Welwyn Rd., Hertford.

East Midlands (Derbyshire, Leicestershire, Lincolnshire, Northamptonshire, Nottinghamshire).
Nottingham Kayak Club:
c/o J. Oliver, 9 Ann's Close, Off Kenrick Road, Mapperley, Nottingham, NG3 6DB.

West Midlands (Herefordshire, Salop, Staffordshire, Warwickshire, Worcestershire).
Birmingham Canoe Club:
c/o A. R. Gosling, 6 Ferndale Park, Pedmore, Stourbridge, West Midlands.
Birmingham Schools Canoe Association:
c/o M. J. Baines, 71 Woodcote Rd., Erdington, Birmingham, B24 0AH.
Emscote Lawn Canoe Club:
c/o J. H. Riley, Emscote Lawn, Warwick.
Royal Leamington Spa Canoe Club:
c/o D. Olorenshaw, 44 Lindsay Crescent, Kenilworth, Warwickshire.
Shrewsbury Canoe Club: c/o P. J. Jarrett, "The Barracks", Cardington, Church Stretton, Salop.
Telford Canoe Club: c/o R. M. Jones, 15 Ludford Drive, Stirchley Park, Telford, Salop.

North West (Cheshire, Greater Manchester, Lancashire, Merseyside).
Manchester Canoe Club:
c/o C. M. Rothwell, 21 Windsor Road, Clayton Bridge, Manchester, M10 6QQ.
Sefton District Canoe Club:
c/o Mrs. C. Allcutt, 4 Redgate, Formby, Nr. Liverpool.

Yorkshire and Humberside
Leeds Canoe Club:
c/o S. Hope, 22 Wrenbury Crescent, Leeds, LS16 7EG.
Sheffield Canoe Club:
c/o K. A. Maslen, The Hall Bungalow, White Edge Drive, Baslow, Bakewell, Derbyshire, DE4 1SJ.
York Canoe Club:
c/o G. M. Shaw, 60 Slessor Road, Foxwood Hill, Acomb, York, YO2 3JG.

Northern (Cleveland, Cumbria, Co. Durham, Northumberland, Tyne & Wear).
Carlisle Canoe Club:
c/o G. Fletcher, 6 Low Moorlands, Dalston, Carlisle.
Lakeland Canoe Club:
c/o Christopher Whiteside, 92 Windermere Rd., Kendal, Cumbria.
Tees Kayak Club:
c/o H. L. Smith, 1 Draycott Avenue, Brookfield, Middlesborough.

Scotland
Edinburgh White Water Club:
c/o Mrs. C. Linn, 50 King's Road, Edinburgh, EH15 1DX.
Madras College Canoe Club:
c/o C. M. Armstrong, Madras College, South Street, St. Andrews, Fife.

Wales
Croesyceiliog Canoe Club:

c/o Mrs. V. Baker, 20 Larkfield Close, Caerleon, Gwent, NP6 1EX.
County of South Glamorgan Canoe Club:
c/o F. J. Adams, Room 114, Education Offices, Kingsway, Cardiff.
North Wales Canoe Club:
Plas T. I., Dolwyddelan, Gwynedd.

Channel Islands
Jersey Canoe Club:
c/o Anthony Ferroro, Studio 18, 23a Beresford St., St. Helier, Jersey.

Clubs without Geographical Boundaries
Canadian Canoe Association of Gt. Britain:
c/o L. H. Rowe, Gable Cottage, Dolons Lane, Leatherhead, Surrey, KT22 8JJ.

Welsh Canoeing Association

Arising from enthusiasm within the Welsh Sports Council and drive from a group of Welsh canoeists, the Welsh Canoeing Association was inaugurated in 1976 and recognised by the B.C.U., as the governing body for the sport of canoeing in Wales.

There is reciprocal membership of the B.C.U. and the W.C.A. with one annual membership fee for those canoeists living in Wales. The development of the association is at an early stage but an active executive committee, similar in size to that of the B.C.U. but responsible for a much smaller geographical area is an essential ingredient for progress.

Appendix 2

The British Canoe Manufacturers Association

A. C. Canoe Products (Chester) Ltd:
P.O. Box 62, Chester — 0244-25277.

Avoncraft:
Burrowfield, Welwyn Garden City, Herts — 07073-30000.

Canoe Centre/Kirton Kayaks Ltd:
Marsh Lane, Crediton, Devon — Crediton 3295.

Cymru Canoes:
St. Hilarys Rd., Llandudno, LL30 1PU — 0492-77067.

Gaybo Ltd: 4 Rose Hill, Brighton, Sussex — 0273-684599.

Granta Boats Ltd:
23 Great Whyte, Ramsey, Huntingdon, Cambs. — 04871-3777.

Harishok Ltd:
Unit 3, Clarendon Trading Estate, Hyde, Cheshire — 061-368-9216.

Howarth Sports:
27 Limefield Rd., Smithills, Bolton, Lancs — 0204-382500.

Jaycee Glassfibre Products:
69 Knights Hill, West Norwood, SE27 — 01-670 1234.

Jon Hyland:
42 Diddington Lane, Hampton in Arden, Solihull, Warks — 067-55 2247.

Lendal Products Ltd:
18/20 Boyd St., Prestwick, Ayrshire — 0292-78558.

P. & H. Fibreglass:
76 Dale Rd., Spondon, Derby — Ilkeston 3155.

Pyranha Mouldings Ltd:
Osnath Works, Lythgoes Lane, Warrington — 0925-31484.

Topcraft Ltd:
324A Birmingham Rd., Walsall, Staffs — 0922-28329.

Trylon Ltd:
Thrift St., Wollaston, Wellingborough, Northants — Wollaston 275.

Tyne Canoes Ltd:
117 St. Margarets Rd., Twickenham, Middx — 01-892 4033.

Valley Canoe Products Ltd:
Private Road 4, Colwick Estate, Nottingham — 0602-249371.

Wet Suits

Aquaquipment:
69 Hatfield Road, St. Albans, Herts.

Insports:
31-39 High Bridge, Newcastle on Tyne.

Vancleeve:
120 Brayards Road, Peckham, SE15.

Trailers

Mechanical Services:
Belmont Road, Bolton.
Or several canoe manufacturers from the Association.